The Country Kitchen
CHUTNEYS & PICKLES
Barbara Beckett

The Country Kitchen

CHUTNEYS & PICKLES

Barbara Beckett

Bloomsbury Books
London

Front and back of jacket: An attractive harvest of autumn vegetables. Ingredients for pumpkin and tomato chutney (p.26), which is cooking on an old wood burning stove. In the background are pickled turnips (p.46) and bread and butter pickles (p.34).

Page 2: Apricot and date chutney can be a delicious accompaniment to a hot spicy meal. This chutney has a particularly nice colour and texture.

 COOK'S NOTES: Standard spoon measurements are used in all recipes.
All spoon measurements are level.
1 tablespoon = 15 ml spoon
1 teaspoon   = 5 ml spoon

As the imperial and metric equivalents are not exact, follow either one or other system of measurement.
All ovens should be preheated to the specified temperature.
Fresh herbs are used unless otherwise stated. If they are unavailable, use half the quantity of dried herbs. Use freshly ground black pepper whenever pepper is used; add salt and pepper to taste. Use plain flour unless otherwise stated.

Published by Harlaxton Publishing Ltd
2 Avenue Road, Grantham, Lincolnshire, NG31 6TA, United Kingdom.
A Member of the Weldon International Group of Companies.

First published in 1992.

© Copyright Harlaxton Publishing Ltd
© Copyright design Harlaxton Publishing Ltd

This edition published in 1993 by
Bloomsbury Books
an imprint of
The Godfrey Cave Group
42 Bloomsbury Street, London. WC1B 3QJ
under license from Harlaxton Publishing Ltd.

Publishing Manager: Robin Burgess
Project Coordinator: Barbara Beckett
Designer & Illustrator : Barbara Beckett
Photographer: Ray Jarratt
Editor in United Kingdom: Alison Leach
Typeset in United Kingdom: Seller's, Grantham
Produced in Singapore by Imago

British Library Cataloguing-in-Publication data.
A catalogue record for this book is available from the British Library.
Title: Country Crafts Series: Chutneys & Pickles
ISBN:1 85471 195 4

CONTENTS

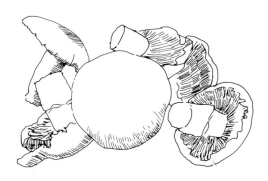

INTRODUCTION

WHAT could be more evocative of country cooking than chutneys and pickles made from summer fruits and vegetables and served with ham, roast meat and curried dishes. I really enjoy chutneys and pickles and their endless variations: the sweetness of apple chutney, the spiciness of pineapple chutney and sour lemon chutney, the sharpness of bread and butter pickles. There is plenty of room for the imagination in chutney and pickle making; so when you have gained confidence, experiment. The endless combinations of spices, fruits and vegetables are fascinating.

Chutneys and pickles are among the easiest things to cook and they have the advantage of lasting for months or even years stored in a dark, dry cupboard. It is always such a pleasure in the middle of winter to open up last summer's pear pickle and enjoy the fruit of your labour. The opened jars also impart perfumes evocative of Asia, the Arab world and the Mediterranean region, the areas where many of the herbs and spices originated.

Besides being easy to make, chutneys and pickles can be made all the year round. I use whatever is in season. If you don't grow your own fruit and vegetables, it is well worth a trip to the markets to buy the best–quality produce at the cheapest prices. I enjoy seeing them in large quantities and attractively displayed. It is often my inspiration as well. I once bought some limes reduced to an almost give–away price. As I was gently rubbing the skin to smell the zest, I noticed some dates. There was my chutney!

Fruit and vegetables are available in a great variety these days. Even during hard times there is usually some item in abundance and cheap enough to buy in a large quantity. By preserving these things you can enjoy them at any time of the year. Chutneys and pickles are very good stand-by's for a quickly prepared meal or when visitors pop in unexpectedly. I love to open my store cupboard and look at my jars of pickled onions, pickled plums, apricot chutney, pear and walnut chutney and pickled peaches. To see them there gives me a great feeling of comfort and anticipated pleasure. Attractively presented, they also make excellent presents for friends and family.

Most of the recipes in this book are for large quantities. You will find half quantities work just as well.

Spiced quinces,
another beautiful looking pickle, makes a lovely
addition to a picnic lunch.

Ingredients

Apples, plums, red and green tomatoes, beetroot, dates, mangoes and rhubarb are the fruits and vegetables commonly used for making chutney. To these are added garlic, onions, chillies, spices, salt, sugar, and vinegar, the last three ingredients being the preservatives. The spices can be tied together in a muslin bag and removed before bottling. I prefer to keep them loose in the chutney.

I generally use a fermented white wine vinegar. However, a good–quality malt vinegar is perfect for some chutneys, such as rhubarb and date chutney. Cider vinegar is excellent.

Use coarse cooking salt, not the free flowing salt that is placed on the table.

Sugar helps to retain the fruit flavour as well as preserve the fruit. I use muscovado sugar or granulated sugar. Castor sugar is just as good. Muscovado gives a darker colour and flavour. You can reduce the amount of sugar used by adding more dried fruits, such as dates, raisins or sultanas, golden syrup, treacle or honey. They will alter the flavour, though, so be careful not to lose the taste of the original fruit.

Hot chillies need careful handling. Be sure not to get seeds under your fingernails or to wipe your eyes while handling chillies. If you aren't experienced, wear fine rubber gloves. Chilli powder can be substituted, but use only a small amount. Chilli sharpens the flavour of any dish wonderfully , but care should be taken not to use too much.

Garlic is one of the most valuable medicinal herbs. It improves the flavour of any savoury dish. Always use the fresh cloves. Throw away the garlic powder.

I always use fresh root ginger. If you haven't a supplier, substitute ground ginger, using half the amount required. Crystallised ginger can also be used, but remember it will add more sugar to the recipe. Ginger adds a sharp tang to chutneys or pickles.

Other commonly used spices in chutneys and pickles are listed below in alphabetical order. They can be used whole, crushed or ground. I grind my own in a food mill, as they taste and smell so much better freshly ground. A coffee mill will grind them satisfactorily, but you should take care in cleaning the mill before and after use, to avoid transferring flavours.

Allspice, has the aroma and taste of cinnamon, cloves and nutmeg, hence its name. The berries from the *Pimenta dioica* tree are used whole, crushed or ground.

Caraway seeds have a very distinctive aromatic taste and flavour. They are also excellent for the digestion. Pickles–and, of course, sauerkraut–are especially well flavoured by caraway seeds.

Cayenne is finely ground dried red chilli pepper. It also has digestive properties. It is very hot and adds an extra depth to the flavour of chutneys or pickles.

Celery seeds are used often in pickles and chutney. They have an excellent flavour and are believed to help rheumatism.

Cinnamon comes from the bark of the tree *Cinnamomum zeylanicum*. It can be used in stick form or ground. Cinnamon has preservative and medicinal qualities and sharpens the flavour of pickles.

Cloves are a powerful antiseptic and add a pungent flavour to dishes. They are used whole or ground.

Coriander seeds have a very nice spicy

COOK'S NOTES: Sharp knives make preparation easy, and they are safer. Keep them clean, dry and sharpened.at all times

This pumpkin and tomato chutney will last a long time if you can resist eating it. The pumpkins and the beautiful red tomatoes are straight from a country garden.

flavour. They can be used whole, crushed or ground in chutneys and pickles.

Fennel seeds are another spice with a very distinctive aromatic taste, as well as being reputed to have many medicinal properties.

Juniper berries give a delicious taste and aroma to food. They are also a digestive and are said to be good for the kidneys. Use whole or crushed.

Mustard seeds are best used whole in chutneys and pickles. They add a pleasant tang to many dishes.

Nutmeg is also a digestive and richly enhances any vegetable or fruit pickle. Freshly grated nutmeg from the large seed is far and away superior to ready ground nutmeg.

Paprika is dried and ground from a red sweet capsicum (pepper). It is excellent as a flavour or a garnish with its beautiful red colour.

Pepper is the king of spices. Always use black pepper for chutneys and pickles. Use whole or freshly ground.

Turmeric is ground from a dried aromatic root (*Curcuma longa*). It is a brilliant yellow colour and adds fragrance and colour to pickles and chutneys.

Chutneys generally simmer for up to two hours, the fruit absorbing the vinegar during this time. When you can draw a wooden spoon across the bottom of the saucepan and there is no runny liquid left, the chutney is ready. As you become familiar with chutney making, you will recognise the sticky thickness that means the chutney is ready for bottling.

It is difficult to give an exact cooking time because the quality of fruit varies. As fruit gets older, it has less ability to absorb sugar. With the exception of red tomatoes, which should be ripe, buy fruit that is slightly under ripe and firm.

It is the long cooking of the sugar which darkens the chutney. If you want a lighter chutney, add white sugar after the fruit has cooked pretty well.

Only heavy–based enamel, or stainless steel saucepan's should be used for cooking chutneys. Use a clean wooden spoon for stirring. Stir occasionally throughout the cooking time, especially towards the end when the chutney is thickening up. It is unwise to leave chutney unattended towards the end of cooking time.

Chutneys should be stored in glass jars. I save all the commercial jars and take the labels off by soaking them or removing the stubborn ones with lighter fluid or. Many of the jars are lovely shapes. Bottle chutney while it is hot in clean jars. Sterilise jars by placing them in a low oven for 30 minutes.

Cover the chutney immediately after putting it into the jars. Chutney reduces in volume if it is not sealed with a dark, efficient seal. Plastic lids are fine, but don't use metal lids unless they have a plastic lining, as the vinegar will eat into the metal and cause spoilage.

Paraffin wax is excellent if you do not have a lid. You can buy it at a pharmacy. Melt it in a small saucepan and pour it over the chutney. You need enough to cover and seal the entire surface.

Make sure the jars are clean outside and inside between the chutney and the top of the jar. another important thing to remember when bottling is to pack the chutney in so there are no air bubbles. Use a spatula to get rid of them; they are breeding grounds for bacteria.

. Never forget to label and date jars of chutney. Having gone to the trouble of making the chutney, it is a shame to waste the time and effort through not knowing what is in the jar and whether it is still good to eat. Chutney is best stored for at least 2 months before opening. Most chutneys will last up to 2 years. You will be amazed how the chutney matures in flavour. Once a jar is opened, refrigerate.

Microwave Cooking

Chutneys can be made very fast in the microwave. I have included some recipes on page 29. The general rule to convert the other chutney recipes for microwave cooking is to put all the ingredients into a large suitable bowl, cover and cook on the highest setting for 30 to 40 minutes or until thickened. Stir every 10 minutes. Watch very carefully in the last 15 minutes of cooking as it begins to thicken. Do not cook very large quantities of fruit and vegetables. The recipes can be safely halved.

Fresh Chutneys

Refreshing fresh chutneys can be made just a few hours before eating. They generally accompany a curry dish and cool the palate after the spiciness of chilli dishes. Some are excellent as salads or for dipping with vegetables and bread. They are good to have around when you are waiting for the steak to cook on the barbecue.

I always use a low fat yogurt in making them. There are excellent yoghurts available now in conveniently sized containers. Always whisk the yogurt smooth before adding the other ingredients. These fresh chutneys can be fun to experiment with by changing the spices and the herbs and vegetables.

Pickles

Fruit and vegetables are preserved, or pickled, by gently cooking in a sweet spiced vinegar. Again, salt, sugar and vinegar are the preservatives. The vegetables and fruit should be fresh and almost ripe, with no blemishes.

Pickles should always be stored in sterilised jars to within 2.5 cm (1 in.) of the top. The brine should cover all the fruit or vegetables. check for air bubbles and dispel them, then seal the jars immediately. Metal lids should not be used unless lined with plastic, but glass lids are suitable. For further details, see the information on cooking and bottling chutney.

Covering the Jars

I make brown paper or fabric covers for the jars and glue them onto the lid. You can trace a circle onto your material from a saucer. After you glue it on, tie a ribbon or even kitchen string around it. Have a selection of labels ready. I like to make my own; I have scattered a few through this book which you could copy. Sometimes I use a tartan theme or cut up an old Liberty blouse and make covers with matching ribbons. Black tissue paper with gold ribbon looks very dramatic. For Christmas I used a handmade red paper, green ribbon and some holly.

CHUTNEYS

Apple Chutney

A lovely chutney with pork and ham, hot or cold. Excellent in a sandwich too with any meat or cheese.

1.5 kg   (3 lb) cooking apples, finely chopped
500 g   (1 lb) onions, finely chopped
250g   (8 oz) sugar
125 ml   (4 fl oz) water
2   tablespoons chopped root ginger
1   teaspoon ground cinnamon
3   red chillies
1/2   tablespoon salt
375   ml (12 fl oz) vinegar

Combine all the ingredients and bring to the boil. Simmer until the mixture thickens and ladle into sterilised jars. Seal straight away, label, and store for 3 months before opening.

Apple & Plum Chutney

This chutney goes very well with hot or cold pork as well as curried dishes.

250 g	(8 oz) sugar
1	teaspoon salt
1	teaspoon ground cinnamon
2	cloves
1	chilli
500 ml	(16 fl oz) white wine vinegar
5	cooking apples, peeled and chopped
10	plums, stoned and chopped
2	onions, chopped
60 g	(2 oz) fresh ginger, chopped
90 g	(3 oz) sultanas

Put the sugar, salt and spices into a saucepan with the vinegar and bring to the boil. Add the apples, plums, onions, ginger and sultanas, then simmer gently for about 1 1/2 hours until it is thick but still a bit runny. Put the chutney into hot sterilised jars, seal and label.

Apple & Tomato Chutney

Use either green or red tomatoes in this recipe.

375 g	(12 oz) sugar
375 ml	(12 fl oz) white vinegar
1	teaspoon ground ginger
1	teaspoon ground allspice
1	teaspoon ground black pepper
1	chilli
1	teaspoon salt
6	medium tomatoes, skinned and chopped
3	cooking apples, chopped
1	onion, chopped
4	cloves garlic, chopped
90 g	(3 oz) sultanas
90 g	(3 oz) prunes, chopped

Make apple chutney when apples are cheap in the shops. I use Granny Smith's for cooking.

Put the sugar, vinegar and spices into a saucepan and bring to the boil. Add the rest of the ingredients and simmer slowly for about 1 1/4 hours or until the mixture begins to thicken. Ladle into hot sterilised jars and cover.

Apricot & Date Chutney

Dried apricots make great chutney. If you want to mature this chutney, you will have to hide it. It is so popular in my home that it seems to disappear as soon as I make it.

500 g	(1 lb) dried apricots, roughly chopped
250 g	(8 oz) sultanas
375 ml	(12 fl oz) white wine vinegar
125 g	(4 oz) brown sugar
250 g	(1/2 lb) chopped dates
1 1/2	tablespoons preserved stem ginger, chopped
250 ml	(8 fl oz) water
1	tablespoon salt
1 1/2	teaspoons mustard seeds
1/2	teaspoon chilli powder

Cover the apricots with water and leave to soak for 1 hour; drain. Place in a saucepan with the sultanas and vinegar, bring slowly to the boil, and simmer for 15 minutes.

Stir in the remaining ingredients, and simmer until thickened. Pour into hot sterilised jars, seal and label.

Apricot & Orange Chutney

Ham and smoked tongue are particularly good with this delicious chutney.

500 g	*(1 lb) dried apricots*
4	*oranges*
2	*onions, thinly sliced*
3	*cloves garlic crushed and chopped*
1	*tablespoon allspice berries, bruised*
2	*tablespoons coriander seeds, crushed*
2	*tablespoons brown mustard seeds*
2	*cloves*
250 g	*(8 oz) sultanas*
500 g	*(1 lb) sugar*
2	*tablespoons chopped fresh ginger*
1	*tablespoon salt*
1.1 ltrs	*(2 pints) white wine vinegar*

Soak the apricots for 1 hour; drain. Boil the oranges for 5 minutes, thinly pare the skin, and cut into thin strips. Remove the pith and chop the pulp. Tie up the allspice, coriander, mustard seeds and cloves in a muslin bag.

Put all the ingredients into a saucepan, bring to the boil, and then simmer for about 1 1/2 hours or until the mixture thickens. Remove the muslin bag and spoon the chutney into sterilised jars. Seal and label immediately.

It is a personal preference whether you take the spices out in the muslin bag. I am just as happy leaving the spices in the chutney, not in the bag, of course.

Beetroot Chutney

A good chutney with cold pickled pork or corned beef. It has a beautiful colour and is excellent as a relish in sandwiches.

1 kg	*(2 lb) cooked beetroot*
500 g	*(1 lb) onions*
500 g	*(1 lb) sugar*
1	*teaspoon allspice berries, crushed*
1	*teaspoon mustard seeds*
1	*teaspoon coriander seeds*
5	*peppercorns*
1	*tablespoon salt*
500 ml	*(16 fl oz) vinegar*
60 g	*(2 oz) flour*

To cook the beetroot, cut off all except 5 cm (2 in.) of the tops, place the beetroot in a large saucepan, cover with water and simmer until tender. Remove skins when cool enough to handle.

Finely chop the beetroot and onions. This can be done in a food processor, best done in several lots; use the pulse action, as the vegetables must not be reduced to a purée, just finely chopped.

Combine the beetroot and onion with the sugar, allspice, mustard seeds, coriander seeds, peppercorns, salt and enough vinegar to cover. Bring to the boil, and gently cook for about 25 minutes.

Mix the flour to a smooth paste with cold water. Add to the beetroot, stirring to thicken, and boil for approximately 5 minutes more.

Pack the chutney into clean, hot jars when cool. Cover and label.

I try to keep a jar of beetroot chutney in the cupboard as it is very handy as a sandwich filler when I have run out of ideas. Try it with cottage cheese, lettuce and a sprinkling of chives.

Celery and tomato chutney goes very well with this appetiser of endive and ham.

Bengal Chutney

A well–known Indian chutney with many variations of ingredients. It can be made without the tomatoes if you prefer. The recipe came from the Bengal Club, echoing the days of the British raj.

6	apples, peeled and chopped
6	tomatoes, skinned and chopped
2	onions, chopped
875 ml	(28 fl oz) brown malt vinegar
155 g	(5 oz) raisins
3	cloves garlic
3	fresh chillies
1	tablespoon mustard seeds
60 g	(2 oz) root ginger grated
1	tablespoon salt
28 g	(9 oz) sugar

Combine the apples, tomatoes, onions and vinegar in the saucepan. Simmer for about 15 minutes or until the onions and apples are soft. Cool, then add the remaining ingredients. Simmer until it is thick and sticky, about 45 minutes. Ladle into hot sterilised jars, then seal and label.

This chutney improves with ageing. Keep for 3 months before opening.

Blackberry Chutney

Chutneys always taste better if you have gathered the fruit yourself, and it is so enjoyable to be eating the harvest of summer in the depth of winter.

1.5 kg	(3 lb) blackberries
500 g	(1 lb) cooking apples, peeled and chopped
500 g	(1 lb) onions, finely chopped
1/2	tablespoon salt
1	tablespoon mustard seeds
1	tablespoon ground ginger
1	tablespoon ground mace
1/4	teaspoon cayenne
500 g	(1 lb) soft brown sugar
1.5 ltrs	(2 3/4 pints) white wine vinegar

Combine all the ingredients in a saucepan and bring to the boil. Simmer for about 1 hour or until thick. Spoon into sterilised jars, cover and label.

Capsicum (Sweet Pepper) & Tomato Chutney

The spices can be put into a muslin bag and removed after cooking if you prefer not to have the whole spices in the chutney.

1.5 kg	(3 lb) tomatoes, skinned and roughly chopped
5	large red peppers (capsicums) seeded and cut into large pieces
500 g	(1 lb) cooking apples, peeled and chopped
3	onions, finely chopped
1	tablespoon salt
750 g	(1 1/2 lb) sugar
1.5 ltrs	(2 3/4 pints) white vinegar
1	tablespoon allspice berries, crushed
1	tablespoon mustard seeds
5	peppercorns
2	chillies
1	tablespoon freshly grated root ginger

Put all the ingredients into a saucepan and simmer for about 2 hours or until thick. Spoon into sterilised jars, seal and label.

Celery & Tomato Chutney

A very refreshing light chutney, just right to eat on a hot summer's night with a cold poached chicken.

1	head celery, chopped
6	tomatoes, skinned and chopped
1	chilli, chopped
250 g	(8 oz) sugar
1	tablespoon salt
1	teaspoon mustard seeds
1	teaspoon allspice berries, crushed
3	cloves, ground
250 ml	(8 fl oz) vinegar

Combine all the ingredients in a saucepan, bring to the boil, and simmer for about an hour or until thick. Ladle into sterilised jars, seal and label.

 COOK'S NOTES: Scrub or gently wash all the fruit and vegetables before cooking.

Chayote Chutney

Chayotes (chokos) are now obtainable from some large supermarkets and oriental food stores. Use them to make this nice old–fashioned chutney with a slight bite to it. Add more chillies if you want it hotter.

3   *chayotes peeled and diced*
2   *cooking apples, peeled and chopped*
2   *onions, chopped*
4   *cloves garlic, finely chopped*
1   *tablespoon grated fresh ginger*
1   *teaspoon mustard seeds*
1   *teaspoon fennel seeds*
2   *chillies, chopped*
3   *cloves*
90 g   *(3 oz) sultanas*
250 g   *(8 oz) soft brown sugar*
375 ml *(12 fl oz) malt vinegar*
1   *tablespoon salt*

Put all the ingredients into a large saucepan and simmer for about an hour or until the chutney thickens. Spoon it into sterilised jars, seal and label.

Lemon Chutney

This is a delicious chutney eaten with hot, spicy dishes. It also has an affinity with lamb.

4   *medium-sized lemons*
4   *medium-sized onions, chopped*
185 g   *(6 oz) sultanas*
185 g   *(6 oz) raisins*
3   *chillies, finely chopped*
500 g   *(1 lb) sugar*
750 ml *(24 fl oz) white vinegar*

Pare the rind thinly off the lemons, and chop it finely. Then squeeze the lemons for the juice. Combine all the ingredients in a bowl, and leave to stand for a few hours. Put the mixture into a saucepan, simmer until chutney is thick and sticky. Ladle into sterilised jars and seal.

Lemon & Mustard seed Chutney

5   *lemons, sliced*
3   *onions, sliced*
185 g   *(6 oz) sultanas*
1   *teaspoon allspice berries, crushed*
2   *bay leaves, crushed and torn*
1   *tablespoon mustard seeds*
500 g   *(1 lb) sugar*
1   *tablespoon salt*
625 ml *(1 pint) cider vinegar*

Be sure to discard all the pips from the lemon slices. Sprinkle the slices with salt and leave them in a colander for 24 hours, then wash them.

Combine all the ingredients in a saucepan and bring to the boil. Simmer for about 40 minutes or until it thickens. Ladle into sterilised jars, seal, and store in a dark cupboard. Try in 6 weeks.

Lime & Date Chutney

This is another chutney that harmonises well with Indian dishes. You may like to use fewer or more chillies. This recipe can also be used with lemons.

10	red chillies
1	tablespoon mustard seeds
500 ml	(16 fl oz) vinegar
6	limes, each cut into 16 pieces
500 g	(1 lb) dates, pitted
185 g	(6 oz) raisins
10	cloves garlic, finely chopped
2	tablespoons finely chopped root ginger
375 g	(12 oz) sugar

Soak the chillies and mustard seeds in the vinegar for 2 hours. Combine all the ingredients in a saucepan and bring to the boil. Slowly simmer for about 45 minutes or until it is thick and sticky. Ladle into sterilised jars, seal and store in a dark, dry cupboard.

Chayote and apple chutney with cheddar cheese and corn bread make a tasty lunch.

Mango Chutney

The most popular of all chutneys and wonderful with cold chicken. Use mangoes that are just ripe. According to old Indian recipes, these chutneys were not cooked; the fruit, onions, salt, spices, sugar and vinegar were mixed in jars, corked down, stirred occasionally, and left out in the sun for about two weeks until matured.

6	large mangoes
	Salt
6	cloves garlic, chopped
500 g	(1 lb) sugar
2	apples, peeled and chopped
375 g	(12 oz) sultanas
1	tablespoon mustard seeds
1	tablespoon finely chopped root ginger
500 ml	(16 fl oz) wine vinegar
6	red chillies, finely chopped

Wipe the mangoes, peel and slice them, remove the stones. Sprinkle them with some salt. Leave for 24 hours in a warm place. Wash, and discard excess liquid.

Bruise the sliced mangoes – this helps to soften them if they are green. Place the remaining ingredients in a saucepan. Stir over low heat until the sugar is dissolved. Add the sliced mangoes, and cook for 30 minutes or until the chutney is thick.

Ladle into sterilised jars, and cover. when cool, label and store in a cool cupboard.

Mango chutney–a perfect accompaniment to coriander chicken and spicy rice.

Marrow & Apple Chutney

2 kg	(4 lb) marrow, peeled and chopped into small pieces
1 kg	(2 lb) cooking apples, peeled and chopped
3	onions, finely chopped
500 g	(1 lb) sugar
1 1/2	tablespoons salt
1	teaspoon chopped chillies
1	tablespoon chopped root ginger
1	tablespoon black peppercorns
1	tablespoon allspice, bruised
1.5 ltrs	(2 3/4 pints) vinegar

Place the marrow in a bowl, sprinkling salt as you layer it. Leave for 24 hours, drain, and wash well.

Put the marrow in a saucepan along with the rest of the ingredients, bring to the boil and simmer until the chutney thickens. Spoon it into sterilised jars, seal, and store for at least 4 weeks before opening.

Orange Chutney

Store this chutney for two months and you will be rewarded with an excellent mature chutney. It goes well with any curry. Try it also with cold duck or chicken.

5	oranges
3	cooking apples, peeled and chopped
185 g	(6 oz) raisins
2	tablespoons grated fresh ginger
3	red chillies, chopped
1	tablespoon salt
5	peppercorns, crushed
5	allspice berries, crushed
375 g	(12 oz) sugar
375 ml	(12 fl oz) white vinegar

Pare the oranges with a potato peeler and finely chop the peel. Remove the pith and pips, chop the flesh. Combine all the ingredients in saucepan, bring to the boil, and simmer for about an hour or until it thickens. Spoon the chutney into hot sterilised jars, seal and label.

Peach Chutney

Dried peaches can be used instead for this delicately flavoured chutney. Use 500 g (1 lb) of dried peaches, soaked in water for several hours.

1 kg	(2 lb) peaches, peeled and sliced
3	onions, finely chopped
500 ml	(16 fl oz) vinegar
250 g	(8 oz) sugar
1	tablespoon allspice berries, crushed
1	tablespoon cloves
1	tablespoon coriander seeds
3	bay leaves
5	chillies, chopped
1	tablespoon finely chopped root ginger
12	pepper corns, crushed

Combine all the ingredients in a saucepan, and boil for about 20 minutes or until the mixture thickens. Spoon into heated jars and seal. Keep refrigerated after you have opened the jar.

Pear & Walnut Chutney

This chutney is delicious with cheese. It makes a very good sandwich filling with cheddar cheese and lettuce.

1.5 kg	(3 lb) pears, peeled and chopped
125 g	(4 oz) walnuts, chopped
2	large cooking apples, peeled and chopped
185 g	(6 oz) sultanas
1	tablespoon chopped fresh ginger
1	teaspoon allspice berries, bruised
1	teaspoon coriander seeds
2	red chillies
250 g	(8 oz) sugar
375 ml	(12 fl oz) wine vinegar

Combine all the ingredients in a saucepan and bring slowly to the boil, stirring occasionally. Simmer for about an hour or until the chutney thickens and you can draw a wooden spoon through it without any running liquid. Ladle into sterilised jars, label, and store for at least 4 weeks before opening.

Pineapple Chutney

If you can resist eating this chutney for a month, you will be well rewarded. It matures wonderfully after 3 months.

250 ml	(8 fl oz) white wine vinegar
250 g	(8 oz) sugar
2	teaspoons salt
1 1/2	tablespoons finely chopped fresh ginger
1	teaspoon ground cinnamon
2	chillies (or to taste)
2	cloves garlic, finely chopped
250 g	(8 oz) diced fresh pineapple
2	Granny Smith apples, peeled and cut into pieces
90 g	(3 oz) raisins

Put the vinegar, sugar, salt, ginger, cinnamon,

chillies and garlic in a saucepan and bring to the boil. Add the pineapple, apples and raisins. Boil slowly, stirring often, until the apple is broken up and the chutney is thick. The pineapple will remain in pieces. Pour into warm jars and seal.

Pineapple chutney is delicious with cold meats and spicy Indian dishes. It has a particularly pleasant texture.

Overleaf: Lime and date chutney is wrapped up and ready to be given as a Christmas present.

Plum Chutney

Damsons, if you are lucky enough to grow them, can be substituted for plums.

1	tablespoon salt
1	teaspoon ground cloves
1	teaspoon mustard seeds
1	teaspoon ground ginger
1	teaspoon ground allspice
2	red chillies
750 ml	(24 fl oz) white wine vinegar
1 kg	(2 lb) plums, stoned

185 g	(6 oz) apple, peeled and sliced
185 g	(6 oz) onions, sliced
125 g	(4 oz) sultanas
125 g	(4 oz) carrot, shredded
500 g	(1 lb) sugar

Put the salt, spices and vinegar in a saucepan and bring slowly to the boil. Add the remaining ingredients and stir until the mixture comes to the boil. Simmer until it thickens. Spoon into sterilised jars, seal and label. Store for 2 months before opening.

Lime and Date Chutney

Lime Chutney
~ tart ~

Prune Chutney

1 kg	(2 lb) prunes
500 g	(1 lb) onions, finely chopped
1	tablespoon chopped root ginger
1/2	teaspoon cayenne
1	tablespoon mustard seeds
1	teaspoon coriander seeds
1	teaspoon black pepper seeds
1	teaspoon allspice
750 ml	(24 fl oz) malt vinegar
500 g	(1 lb) sugar

Soak prunes for 1 day in just enough water to cover them. Drain, remove stones, and chop.

Combine all the ingredients in a saucepan and simmer until the mixture thickens. Put at once into sterilised jars, seal, and store in a dark place.

Remember that chutneys are best if cooked so they are still a bit runny; if they are too solid they dry up too quickly.

Pumpkin & Tomato Chutney

This is one of the most beautiful chutneys I have ever made. The colours of the pumpkin and tomato are glorious, fading from their original colours to warm reds and oranges.

1.25 kg	(2 1/2 lb) pumpkin, peeled and cut into large bite–sized pieces
6	tomatoes, skinned and chopped
3	onions, chopped
185 g	(6 oz) raisins
500 g	(1 lb) sugar
1	tablespoon salt
2	tablespoons chopped root ginger
12	black peppercorns
1	tablespoon allspice berries, crushed
4	cloves garlic, crushed and chopped
1 litre	(1 3/4 pints) white vinegar

Put all the ingredients into a saucepan, bring to the boil, simmer until the mixture thickens,

Rhubarb and dates, an excellent combination for a spicy chutney, which is served here with chicken in white wine and Persian rice salad.

which should take about 50 minutes. This chutney needs to be stirred towards the end, as it is inclined to get sticky. Spoon into sterilised jars, seal and label.
This chutney keeps well and tastes much nicer after several months.

Rhubarb & Date Chutney

This chutney has a lovely colour and goes very well with cold pork or corned beef.

2 kg	*(4 lb) rhubarb, chopped*
500 g	*(1 lb) dates, pitted and chopped*
500 g	*(1 lb) onions, finely chopped*
1	*tablespoon grated root ginger*
1	*tablespoon allspice berries, crushed*
1	*tablespoon coriander seeds, crushed*
6	*black peppercorns, crushed*
2	*chillies*
2	*bay leaves, crushed*
1	*tablespoon salt*
750 g	*(1 1/2 lb) sugar*
1.1 litre	*(2 pints) vinegar*

Combine all the ingredients in a saucepan, bring to the boil, and simmer for 2 hours or until the mixture thickens. (If a spoon is drawn through, it shouldn't leave any running liquid.) Ladle into sterilised jars, seal and label.

ALTERNATIVE: This chutney turns a lovely rich maroon colour. To make it lighter, use white vinegar and put the sugar in after an hour's cooking.

 COOK'S NOTES: Runny liquid on the top of chutney means the chutney hasn't absorbed the vinegar properly and needs more cooking.

Green Tomato Chutney

This is a very hot chutney, but it is worth while trying as it is delicious.

2 kg	*(4 lb) green tomatoes, peeled and chopped*
500 g	*(1 lb) apples, peeled and chopped*
4	*medium onions*
155 g	*(5 oz) dates, pitted and chopped*
185 g	*(6 oz) sultanas*
2	*tablespoons chopped root ginger*
15	*red chillies*
500 g	*(1 lb) sugar*
1	*tablespoon salt*
750 ml	*(24 fl oz) vinegar*

Place all the ingredients in a large saucepan. Bring to the boil and simmer for about 2 hours or until the chutney thickens. Spoon into sterilised jars, seal and label. Store in a cool, dark cupboard.

Mild Green Tomato Chutney

Mild green tomato chutney has always been a great favourite in our family. It is definitely worth a trip to the markets to get the green tomatoes if you don't grow your own.

1 kg	*(2 lb) cooking apples, peeled and chopped*
3	*medium onions, finely chopped*
6	*cloves garlic, finely chopped*
375 g	*(12 oz) raisins*
2 kg	*(4 lb) green tomatoes, roughly chopped*
2	*tablespoons finely chopped root ginger*
2	*tablespoons mustard seeds*
6	*allspice berries, crushed*
1/2	*teaspoon chopped dry chilli*
750 g	*(1 1/2 lb) sugar*
1	*tablespoon salt*
1 litre	*(1 3/4 pints) vinegar*

Combine all the ingredients in a large saucepan, bring to the boil, and simmer for about 3 hours, stirring frequently, especially towards the end. When it is thickening and you can take a wooden spoon through it without any running liquid, it is done. Ladle into sterilised jars, seal and store.

Tomato Chutney

This recipe comes from a friend in India. Not only is it wonderful with curries, but it goes very well with cold poultry.

2 kg	(4 lb) tomatoes, peeled and roughly chopped
20	cloves garlic, roughly chopped
2	tablespoons chopped root ginger
90 g	(3 oz) raisins
375 g	(12 oz) sugar
1	tablespoon salt
2	chillies
	Zest and juice of 1 lemon
1/2	teaspoon cumin seeds
1/2	teaspoon fennel seeds
1/2	teaspoon fenugreek
375 ml	(12 fl oz) white wine vinegar

Combine all the ingredients in a saucepan, bring to the boil, and simmer for about 1 1/2 to 2 hours, stirring frequently, or until the chutney is thick. The cooking time depends on how firm the tomatoes are; if they are watery, it will take longer to cook. Spoon into sterilised jars, seal, and store in a dark, dry cupboard.

Tomato chutney dressed up ready to be put under the Christmas tree. By making chutneys and jams through the year you will give yourself an easier and more economical Christmas.

MICROWAVE CHUTNEYS

These recipes are tantalisingly fast to make. Chutneys thicken at the end of cooking and need watching carefully.

Date & Apple Chutney

750 g   (1 1/2 lb) cooking apples,
         peeled, cored and chopped
500 g   (1 lb) dates, pitted and chopped
250 g   (8 oz) onions, finely chopped
375 g   (12 oz) soft brown sugar
125 g   (4 oz) sultanas
1   teaspoon salt
1   teaspoon ground ginger
2   cloves garlic, chopped
1/2   teaspoon cayenne
625 ml (1 pint) white wine vinegar

Place all the ingredients in a large bowl, cover and cook on a high setting for 35 to 45 minutes or until thickened, stir every 10 minutes.

Leave to cool slightly, then ladle into sterilised jars. Cover, seal and label and store in a dark cupboard.

COOK'S NOTES: Fruit and vegetables are important sources of vitamin C, among other vital nutrients. It is important that the goodness is preserved when you cook them. Care should be taken that the fruit and vegetables used are fresh and preparation is as fast as possible. Don't soak them in water for a long time.

Tomato Chutney

750 g   (1 1/2 lb) tomatoes,
         skinned and quartered
250 g   (8 oz) onions, finely chopped
185 g   (6 oz) soft brown sugar
125 g   (4 oz) sultanas
1   teaspoon salt
1   teaspoon ground allspice
1   teaspoon mustard seeds, ground
2   chillies, chopped
315 ml (1/2 pint) malt vinegar

Place all the ingredients in a large bowl, cover and cook on the highest setting for 35 to 45 minutes or until thickened, stirring every 10 minutes.

Leave to cool slightly, then ladle into sterilised jars. Cover, seal and label and store in a cool cupboard.

Rhubarb Chutney

500 g   (1 lb) rhubarb, chopped
500 g   (1 lb) dates, pitted and chopped
1   large onion, chopped
185 g   (6 oz) soft brown sugar
315 ml (1/2 pint) wine vinegar
2   teaspoons chopped root ginger
1   teaspoon ground ginger
1   chilli, chopped

Place all the ingredients in a very large bowl and mix well. Cover and cook on the highest setting for about 30 minutes or until thickened, stirring every 10 minutes.

Leave to cool slightly, ladle into sterilised jars. Cover, seal and label in the usual way.

FRESH CHUTNEYS

Fresh Apple & Mint Chutney

This refreshing chutney needs to be made only a few hours before serving. Serve it in a small bowl to accompany Indian food. It is a great favourite at barbecues.

30 g	(1 oz) fresh mint leaves
2	tablespoons lemon juice
2	red chillies
1	green apple, peeled and diced (keep it in the lemon juice)
1	orange, peeled, seeded and cubed
1	teaspoon salt

Combine all the ingredients in a blender and blend to a smooth paste. Cover and refrigerate until serving.

VARIATION: I have made this with coriander leaves instead of mint, with delicious results. Sometimes I add a little coriander seed and cumin which has been roasted and freshly ground.

Coriander Chutney

A cool relish to serve with a hot curry meal.

30 g	(1 oz) fresh coriander chopped
1	hot green chilli
1/2	teaspoon salt
1	teaspoon roasted cumin seeds, ground
1	tablespoon lemon or lime juice
1	tablespoon grated root ginger
250 ml	(8 fl oz) natural yogurt

Put all the ingredients except the yogurt into a food processor and blend to a smooth paste. Put the yogurt into a bowl and whisk smooth. Fold in the coriander paste with the yogurt, and refrigerate until ready to serve.

VARIATION: This chutney can also be used as a dip for fresh vegetables as a starter to a meal. Add more yogurt if it is too thick for a dip.

Coconut Chutney

This is a lovely accompaniment to a barbecue or any hot chilli dish.

90 g	(3 oz) desiccated coconut
1	chilli, finely chopped
3	spring onions, finely chopped
1	tablespoon lime or lemon juice
2	tablespoons hot milk
1/2	teaspoon salt

Mix all the ingredients together and serve in a small bowl accompanied by a bowl of fresh coriander or mint.

Fresh Green Chutney

This chutney is delicious with any kind of lamb dish, hot, cold or spicy.

45 g	(1 1/2 oz) mint or coriander leaves
1	green chilli
2	tablespoons lemon juice
2	spring onions, finely chopped
	Pepper
1	teaspoon sugar
1/2	teaspoon salt

Apple and mint chutney, besides being a traditional part of an Indian meal, can be served as a salad accompanying any meat dish.

Blend the coriander and chilli with the lemon juice in a food processor. Combine this paste with the rest of the ingredients in a bowl. Refrigerate until ready to serve later in the day.

VARIATION: Add some fine chopped cucumber.

COOK'S NOTES: *The fruit and vegetables for chutneys and jams don't need to be the finest quality, so buy cheaply. As long as they are firm, sound and unblemished they will be perfect for preservation.*

Sesame Seed Chutney

Chicken and fish taste excellent with this unusual fresh chutney.

6	*tablespoons sesame seeds*
2	*cloves*
3	*spring onions, chopped*
1	*tablespoon finely chopped red pepper (capsicum)*
2	*tablespoons lemon juice*
	A pinch of cayenne
1/2	*teaspoon salt*

Toast the sesame seeds in a dry frying pan until they begin to turn colour. Put them in a food processor with the other ingredients. Blend to a thick paste and refrigerate.

Walnut chutney is a very popular fresh Indian chutney. It makes an excellent appetiser too – just add an extra 125 ml (4 fl oz) yogurt and serve with crudités or crusty bread.

Yogurt Chutney

I love the combination of mint and coriander; it is so refreshing with a hot, spicy meal. I often have this dish as a snack for lunch with some bread and fruit.

Walnut chutney

Walnut chutney seems to go with just about any Indian meal. It is quick and easy to make.

90 g   (3 oz) shelled walnuts
1   red chilli, chopped
*   A pinch of salt*
125 ml (4 fl oz) natural yogurt

Grind the walnuts, chilli and salt in a food mill or food processor until smooth. Whisk the yogurt in a bowl until smooth, then mix in the walnut paste. Refrigerate until ready to serve.

500 ml (16 fl oz) natural yogurt
2   tablespoons finely chopped
*   fresh coriander*
2   tablespoons finely chopped fresh mint
2   tablespoons finely chopped onions
1/2   tablespoon chopped garlic
1   red chilli, chopped
*   A pinch of pepper*
*   A pinch of salt*

Whisk the yoghurt in a bowl until smooth. Mix all other ingredients into the bowl, then refrigerate. Garnish with a few coriander leaves.

PICKLES

Pickling Vinegar

Pickling vinegar can be used to spice chutneys, fruit and vegetables. You can make up a large batch of it and have it on hand for whenever you have a glut of fruit or vegetables. It is made up in many different combinations, but I find the following is the most satisfactory.

1	tablespoon mustard seeds
1	tablespoon coriander seeds
1	tablespoon allspice berries
1	teaspoon peppercorns
1	tablespoon salt
1 to 3	red chillies
2	bay leaves, crushed
	A few pieces of root ginger
2 litres	(3 1/2 pints) white vinegar

Combine all the ingredients in a saucepan, bring to the boil, then simmer for 10 minutes. Spoon into sterilised bottles, seal and label.

You may prefer to tie the spices up in a muslin bag and remove the bag at bottling stage. To make the bottle look more attractive, add, when appropriate, garlic cloves or fennel seed stalks, small celery leaves, beetroot slices to turn the vinegar pink, and herbs. There are endless combinations, and it is fun to experiment. Many of the recipes in this book can be made with the pickling vinegar.

 COOK'S NOTES: To peel vegetables, use a potato peeler. Before skinning tomatoes, pour boiling water on them in a bowl and let them stand for 30 seconds; then cool them under cold running water.

Pickled Beetroot

A favourite pickle with cold meats and salad. Use it chopped as a filling for pitta bread with lettuce, mint and cucumber.

12	medium beetroots
2	tablespoons chopped celery stalks and small leaves
750 ml	(24 fl oz) white vinegar
125 g	(4 oz) sugar
1	tablespoon allspice berries, crushed
3	cloves
12	black peppercorns
3	cloves garlic

Cook the beetroot in boiling water for about 50 minutes or until tender. The timing depends on how big they are. Peel and slice them. Pack into warm sterilised jars with pieces of celery and leaves in between.

In the meantime, put the vinegar, sugar and spices into the saucepan, bring to the boil, and simmer for 5 minutes only. Let the liquid stand for several hours before pouring it, strained, over the beetroot slices. You may omit the standing period if you are not straining off the spices.

 COOK'S NOTES: If the chutney shrinks in the jar after a month, it means it hasn't been covered properly. Chutneys should be sealed with a plastic-lined metal lid or plastic lid. Jam covers and paper covers are not enough to prevent the vinegar evaporating. You can put paper and material covers over the plastic lid to make it more attractive.

Bread & Butter Pickles

Bread and butter pickles are crunchy, juicy and full of flavour, yet easy to make if you follow the instructions. For crisp pickles, select fresh, good quality cucumbers, slightly immature, and pickle them immediately.

2.25 kg (4 1/2 lb) cucumbers,
    sliced 5 mm (1/4 in.) thick
500 g (1 lb) onions, thinly sliced
125 g (4 oz) salt
    Water
    Ice cubes
750g-1 kg (1 1/2 - 2 lb) sugar
1.25 ltr (2 1/4 pints) cider vinegar
    or white vinegar
1 1/2 teaspoons fennel seeds
1 1/2 teaspoons brown mustard seeds
1 1/2 teaspoons turmeric
2 red chillies

In a large bowl, mix together the cucumbers, onions and salt. Cover with cold water and ice cubes and leave for 3 hours. drain, rinse well and drain again. Set aside.

About 30 minutes before the cucumber mixture is ready, combine in a large saucepan the sugar, vinegar, fennel, mustard seeds and turmeric. Stir over medium heat until the sugar has dissolved. Increase the heat and bring to the boil. Reduce the heat and simmer uncovered for 30 minutes or until very syrupy, stirring often.

Meanwhile, sterilise jars and lids. Add cucumbers and onions to the syrup; heat but do not boil, stirring occasionally.

Ladle the hot mixture into hot jars leaving 1cm (1/2 in.) head space. Using a spatula, release any air bubbles from around the side and bottom of each jar. Wipe and close the jars. Store in a cool, dark cupboard; when a jar is opened, store it in the refrigerator.

Pickled Red Cabbage

A beautiful coloured dish on the table and deliciously crunchy.

1   red cabbage, finely shredded
250 g (8 oz) salt
500-750 ml (16-24 fl oz) pickling vinegar
    (p 33)

Be sure to remove the coarse outer leaves of the cabbage and the thick white stalks. Put the shredded cabbage in a large bowl, sprinkling with salt as you put it in. Cover and leave for 24 hours.

Drain and rinse the cabbage. Put into sterilised warm jars and cover with the cold pickling vinegar. Seal and label. It is ready to eat in a week, but don't leave for more than 6 weeks, as it becomes soft.

COOK'S NOTES: Keep chutneys and pickles refrigerated after opening the jars. When taking fruits and chutneys from storage in the refrigerator, leave for 1 hour before eating them.

Bread and butter pickles are a perennial favourite and so handy as a stand-by in the store cupboard. The pickled turnips have a delicate mild flavour and look lovely dyed a pale pink from a few beetroot slices.

Pickled Red Cabbage & Cauliflower

This pickle is a very pretty pale pink, dyed by the red cabbage..

1/2	red cabbage
1	cauliflower
3	tablespoons salt
1 litre	(1 3/4 pints) water
375 ml	(12 fl oz) white vinegar
1	teaspoon caraway seeds
1	red chilli
1	bay leaf

Cut the cabbage into 3 cm (1/4 in) squares. Separate the cauliflower into florets. Pack the vegetables into large sterilised jars, arranging them alternately in layers. Mix the salt, water, vinegar, caraway seeds and chilli together and pour over the vegetables. Seal, label and store. It will be ready to eat in a week, but do not keep it longer than 2 months, as the vegetables will lose their crispness.

Sweet pepper retains its rich colour through the pickling process

Pickled Sweet Peppers (Capsicums)

A glorious rich red dish to enhance any cold collation and lift the spirits.

1 kg	(2 lb) red peppers (capsicums)
3 1/2	tablespoons salt
1 litre	(1 3/4 pints) water
500 ml	(16 fl oz) white vinegar
3	cloves garlic
1	bay leaf
1	tablespoon fennel seeds
90 g	(3 oz) celery stalks and leaves, chopped

Cut the peppers into large pieces, after discarding the seeds and cores. Pack them in a sterilised jar. Mix the other ingredients and pour over the peppers. Seal, label, and store in a dark place. They should be ready to eat in 8 to 10 days. They will deteriorate after about 6 to 7 weeks.

Cabbage & Capsicum Pickle (Csalamade)

A cabbage pickle from Czechoslovakia.

1	small white cabbage, shredded
250 g	(8 oz) salt
3	green peppers (capsicums), thinly sliced
3	onions, cut into thin rings
1 1/2	tablespoons black peppercorns
2	cloves
6	bay leaves
3	cloves garlic
125 g	(4 oz) sugar
375 ml	(12 fl oz) vinegar
375 ml	(12 fl oz) water

Put the cabbage into a large bowl and sprinkle with salt as you go.

Leave for an hour. Wash the cabbage, drain, then add the peppers, onions, peppercorns, cloves, bay leaves, garlic and sugar. Pack the mixture into a sterilised jar then pour over the vinegar followed by the water, right up to the brim. Seal and label. It should be ready to eat in a week or keep for up to 8 weeks.

Pickled Cucumbers

This is a light, delicate pickle from Indonesia.

4	cucumbers
125 g	(4 oz) salt
500-750 ml	(16-24 fl oz) white vinegar
2	tablespoons sugar
3	chillies, chopped

Cut the cucumbers lengthways into four. Scoop out the seeds with a spoon then cut the cucumbers into cubes. Put the cubes into a bowl, sprinkle with salt and cover with water and ice cubes. Leave for 2 hours. Drain and rinse.

Put the vinegar and sugar into a saucepan and bring to the boil. Simmer until the sugar dissolves, then add the cucumbers and chillies. Bring to the boil again, remove from the heat. It is ready to eat as soon as it is cool. It will last up to 2 weeks if bottled and refrigerated.

Dill Pickles

One of the best-loved pickles of all, with the delicate flavouring of dill seeds.

500 g   (1 lb) small pickling cucumbers
2   cloves garlic
2   teaspoon dill seeds
1   teaspoon peppercorns
1   teaspoon coriander seeds
2   bay leaves
250 ml   (8 fl oz) white vinegar
1   tablespoon salt

Wash the cucumbers well and pack them into sterilised jars. Distribute the garlic, dill seeds, peppercorns, coriander seeds and bay leaves around the jar.

Put the vinegar and salt into a saucepan and bring to the boil. Take off the heat and pour into the jars. Seal, label and store in a dark cupboard. They are ready to eat in a week and last about 4 to 6 weeks. Refrigerate once the jar has been opened.

VARIATION: If you can't get the pickling cucumbers, substitute very small cucumbers, or cut large cucumbers into 2 or 4 pieces.

Pickled Aubergine (Eggplant)

Although this recipe calls for baking in a hot oven, it is even better to grill the aubergine over glowing coals. The smoke permeates the flesh and adds a wonderful smoky flavour.

2   medium aubergine (eggplants)
250 ml   (8 fl oz) vinegar
60 ml   (2 fl oz) lemon juice
2   teaspoons mustard seeds
2   teaspoons coriander seeds, toasted
1   teaspoon fennel seeds
3   cloves garlic
2   teaspoons chopped root ginger
          A pinch of chilli powder
          Salt and pepper

Pierce the aubergine all over with a fork and place them on a rack in a preheated hot oven (220°C; 400°F, gas 6) with a dish below to catch juices. Bake for 30 minutes or until soft.

Halve the aubergine lengthways, scoop out the flesh, and chop finely. Mix with 125 ml (4 fl oz) vinegar to prevent discolouration.

Put the lemon juice and the remaining vinegar into a blender with the mustard, coriander and fennel seeds, garlic and ginger, and blend until smooth. Add to aubergine flesh, and season to taste with chilli powder, salt and pepper.

Spoon into sterilised jars and store, covered, in the refrigerator. This savoury purée will keep under refrigeration for several weeks.

Aubergine pickle goes well with a few slices of tomato in a warm crusty roll.

PICKLED
LEMONS 26/8

Ginger Pickle

This Thai ginger pickle is an excellent accompaniment to any Oriental dish. It is very useful if you live in an area where fresh root ginger is not always available.

500 g   (1 lb) root ginger
1   red chilli
250 g   (8 oz) sugar
750 ml   (24 fl oz) white vinegar

Peel the skin off the ginger and slice it thinly. Put the chilli, sugar and vinegar into a saucepan and bring to the boil. Add the ginger and simmer for about 45 minutes. Spoon into sterilised jars, label, and store in a dark cupboard. It will be ready in 1 week.

Honeydew Melon Pickle

This sweet and sour pickle is excellent with all cold meats and also makes a pleasant accompaniment to curries.

A honeydew melon,
cut into 2 cm (3/4 in.) cubes
375 ml (12 fl oz) pickling vinegar (page 33)
500 g   (1 lb) sugar
1   tablespoon grated root ginger
2   cloves garlic, finely chopped

Bring a large saucepan of water to the boil, put in the melon, and as soon as the water comes to the boil again, remove the fruit and plunge it under a cold water tap to refresh.

These pickled lemons taste as good as they look. I love the look of them, and so do my guests.

Bring the vinegar to the boil in a saucepan, put in the melon, and cook for 2 minutes after the vinegar has come to the boil. Pour the melon and vinegar into a large china bowl, cover, and leave for 2 days. It looks dull and cloudy at this stage. It will clear at a second cooking.

Strain off the vinegar, bring it to the boil, add the sugar, ginger and garlic. Now add the melon, boil for 3 minutes, and then take out the melon with a slotted spoon and pack into warm jars. Keep the syrup boiling for a while, removing any scum that has been thrown up. when it has cooled down a bit, pour it over the melon. Try to wait a few weeks before being tempted to open a jar.

Pickled Limes

As well as being a fine accompaniment to curry dishes, these sour limes are delicious finely cut in a salad. I make a salad of watercress, shredded apple and pickled limes with a vinaigrette.

12   limes
125 g   (4 oz) salt
5   bay leaves
1   tablespoon paprika
10   peppercorns
375 ml (12 fl oz) olive oil

Wash the limes and cut them into slices. Sprinkle them with the salt, and leave to drain in a colander for 24 hours.

Pack the lime slices and bay leaves into sterilised jars, sprinkling the paprika and peppercorns between each layer. Cover with olive oil, seal and label. The limes should be ready to eat in 4 weeks.

VARIATION: Lemons are just as good made this way. If they are large lemons, use fewer lemons for this mixture. You may also prefer a lighter flavoured oil.

Do not throw away the oil when you have finished the limes or lemons. It makes a wonderful vinaigrette with a real zest to it. It is good for sautéeing anything that lime or lemon will add a tang to.

Mixed Pickles

There are many variations for mixed pickles. Select some vegetables from the following, as they are all good for pickling: cauliflowers, cucumbers, cabbages, red or green peppers (capsicums), onions, tomatoes, turnips, carrots, and green beans.

1 kg   (2 lb) mixed vegetables
500 ml (16 fl oz) pickling vinegar (page 33)

Trim and peel the vegetables and cut them into small pieces. Pack them into sterilised jars, and pour hot pickling vinegar over them. Seal, label and store. They will be ready to eat in a week. Don't keep them longer than 2 months.

VARIATION: beetroot and red cabbage are also excellent to pickle, especially if you want a nice pink colour. A chilli or two give an extra bite.

 COOK'S NOTES: The term dice means to cut fruit or vegetables into small cubes about 0.5 to 1 cm (1/4 to 1/2 in.). Halve and quarter for fruit and vegetables means to cut in half from top to bottom, then cut in half again, but making the second cut at right angles to the first.

Fresh Pickles

This is a fresh pickle to be eaten straight away. It could last up to a week, bottled and stored in the refrigerator.

500 ml (16 fl oz) vinegar
1   tablespoon salt
1 kg   (2 lb) mixed vegetables; cauliflower, cabbage, cucumbers, carrots, pickling onions, cut into small pieces
1   onion, finely chopped
3   red chillies, finely chopped
3   cloves garlic, finely chopped
1   tablespoon finely chopped root ginger
2   tablespoons oil

Bring the vinegar and salt to the boil, and add the mixed vegetables for 1 minute. Drain.

Mix the onion, chillies, garlic and ginger together. Stir fry in the oil for a few minutes, then add the vegetables and stir fry for a minute. Drain and place in a bowl.

Mint leaves sprinkled on top give the dish for an extra tang.

Pickled Mushrooms

Use only tiny mushrooms. If you can not get them, then halve or quarter large ones.

500 ml (16 fl oz) pickling vinegar (page 33)
1 kg   (2 lb) button mushrooms
1   onion, finely chopped

Bring the picking vinegar to the boil, add the mushrooms and onion, and simmer until mushrooms are tender. Spoon into warm sterilised jars, and pour the vinegar over the mushrooms. Seal, label, and store in a dark place. They will be ready to eat in 2 weeks.

Piccalilli

A great stand–by for sandwiches, home made piccalilli is so much nicer than the commercial varieties. You will never buy them again after you have tasted this recipe.

2 kg	(4 lb) mixed vegetables: cauliflower, onions, green beans, cucumbers and green tomatoes
125 g	(4 oz) salt
250 g	(8 oz) sugar
1	tablespoon dry mustard
1	tablespoon turmeric
750 ml	(24 fl oz) vinegar
3	tablespoons cornflour
3	chillies
1	tablespoon chopped root ginger

Cut the vegetables into small pieces. Put them into a large bowl and sprinkle with salt. Leave for 24 hours, drain, and wash well.

Make a paste by mixing the sugar, mustard, turmeric and cornflour together with a little vinegar. Heat the rest of the vinegar with the chillies; when it comes to the boil, add the vegetables and simmer for 15 minutes.

Remove the vegetables and pack into sterilised jars. Add the paste to the vinegar, stirring for 5 minutes, then pour it over the vegetables.

Seal, label and store in a dark cupboard. It will be ready to eat in a week and will last for a few months.

 COOK'S NOTES: An alternative method for sterilising jars is to put them in the dishwasher without powder and use a hot cycle. This would be a bit extravagant unless you are doing a very large batch of bottling.

Pickled Plums

These plums are delicious with hot lamb chops, especially if you are barbecuing them.

1.5 kg	(3 lb) plums
1	tablespoon finely chopped root ginger
2	red chillies
1	teaspoon ground cloves
1	teaspoon ground cinnamon
2	tablespoons ground allspice
1	tablespoon salt
375 g	(12 oz) sugar
500 ml	(16 fl oz) vinegar

Take the stalks off the plums, wash the fruit and prick with a needle.

Put all the other ingredients into a saucepan and cook slowly until boiling, stirring occasionally. Add the plums and simmer gently for a few minutes. If the plums are too ripe, the skin will break.

Spoon the plums into sterilised jars. Keep boiling the syrup until it thickens, then pour over the plums. Seal, label and store for 2 months before eating.

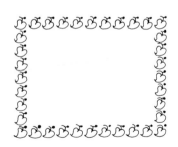

 COOK'S NOTES: If there is cloudy fluid in the pickles, it means either the vegetable brine was insufficient or the spices were not strained from the vinegar. I find the colour attractive.

PICKLED
ORANGE 36/8

Pickled Oranges

4	oranges
	A pinch of bicarbonate of soda
500 ml	(16 fl oz) white vinegar
250 g	(8 oz) sugar
1	teaspoon ground cloves
1	cinnamon stick
6	cloves
4	bay leaves

Scrub the oranges and put in a saucepan with the soda and cover with water. Bring to the boil, then simmer for about 20 minutes. Take the oranges out of the water and cut them into 8 wedges each.

Make a syrup with the vinegar, sugar, ground cloves and cinnamon, stirring until the sugar has dissolved. When it has come to the boil, add the orange wedges. Simmer for 15 minutes.

Place the orange wedges in sterilised jars, add the whole cloves and bay leaves, and pour the syrup over them. Seal and label. They will be ready to eat in a week.

COOK'S NOTES: Most of the recipes in this book are for large quantities. If you halve the quantity the recipe will work just as well.

Pickled oranges are extremely refreshing and excellent with cold duck or chicken.

Pickled Peaches

Eat this fruit pickle with roast turkey – they harmonise wonderfully. If you cannot get small peaches, use larger ones cut in half.

2 kg	(4 lb) small peaches
1	cinnamon stick
1	nutmeg, grated
1	tablespoon finely sliced root ginger
1	teaspoon allspice berries, crushed
750 g	(1 1/2 lb) sugar
750 ml	(24 fl oz) water
750 ml	(24 fl oz) white vinegar
1	tablespoon cloves

Peel the peaches by first pouring boiling water over them; the skin should come off easily after a few minutes. To prevent discolouration, keep the peaches in water with the juice of a lemon until needed.

Put the cinnamon, nutmeg, ginger, allspice, sugar, water and vinegar into a saucepan, then bring to the boil. Simmer for 10 minutes.

Stud each peach with 2 cloves, and put them into the syrup. Simmer until tender. They should only take a few minutes. Pack the peaches into sterilised jars.

Keep boiling the syrup until it begins to thicken, then pour over the peaches. Seal, label and store in a dry cupboard. They will be ready to eat after 6 weeks and even better after 10 weeks.

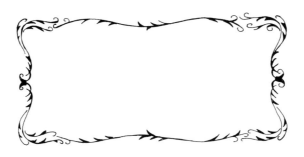

Pickled Pears

These pears taste very good with cheese, especially parmesan cheese.

1 kg	*(2 lb) pears, peeled,*
	cored and quartered
	Juice of half a lemon
1	*tablespoon cloves*
1	*teaspoon allspice berries*
1	*teaspoon coriander seeds*
1	*teaspoon finely sliced root ginger*
1	*cinnamon stick*
1	*piece lemon rind*
500 g	*(1 lb) sugar*
500 ml	*(16 fl oz) vinegar*

When peeling and quartering the pears, place them in a bowl with water and the lemon juice to prevent discolouration. Stud each piece with a clove.

Place the spices, lemon rind, sugar and vinegar in a saucepan. Bring to the boil, and add the pears. Simmer slowly until the pears are tender. Spoon the pears into sterilised jars. Keep cooking the syrup until it thickens; then pour it over the pears.

Seal, label and store. They will be ready to eat in 2 weeks.

Spiced Quinces

If you are lucky enough to have access to some quinces, this is a delicious way of preserving them. it is best to cook them when they turn yellow and have a distinctive scent; they won't absorb the sugar if they are too old.

6	*quinces, peeled,*
	cored and cut into 8 pieces each
1	*tablespoon salt*
375 g	*(12 oz) sugar*
250 ml	*(8 fl oz) white vinegar*
2	*teaspoons coriander seeds*
1	*teaspoon allspice berries*

Cover the quince pieces with water and a tablespoon of salt. Boil for 10 minutes, then strain. You should have three cups of juice.

Add the sugar, vinegar, coriander and allspice to the juice in a saucepan and bring to the boil. Put in the fruit and simmer until it is tender, then remove from the heat and leave in the saucepan for 12 hours.

Drain off the syrup, bring it to the boil, and pour over the quinces placed in sterilised jars. Seal, label, and store in a dark place.

These spiced quinces last a long time. They taste very good with cold poultry or ham.

Make pickled pears when the fruit is cheap.

Pickled Turnips

These are among my favourite pickles. They have such a delicate, subtle flavour and look wonderful in their delicate pale pink brine that is coloured by the beetroot.

1 kg	(2 lb) small white turnips, quartered
	Some celery leaves
4	cloves garlic
2	cloves
10	peppercorns
1	raw beetroot, sliced
3	tablespoons salt
500 ml	(16 fl oz) water
500 ml	(16 fl oz) vinegar

Put the turnips into sterilised jars along with the celery leaves, garlic, cloves, peppercorns and beetroot.

Mix the salt, water and vinegar together and pour over the turnips. Seal, label and store in a warm place.

The turnips will be ready to eat in 10 days. Unfortunately they will keep no longer than about 6 weeks.

INDEX

Page numbers in **bold** type indicate illustrations.